MW00579101

The (NEW) Crunch-Time™ Guide to Parenting Language for Chinese Adoption

The absolute, must-have, can't-live-without-it, English to Chinese words and phrases you need to communicate effectively with your newly adopted child while in China and after you get home.

Hear the actual Chinese pronunciations! Details inside.

By Kat LaMons & Trish Diggins

The New Crunch-Time Guide to
Parenting Language for Chinese Adoption

By Kat LaMons & Trish Diggins

ISBN 978-0-9893732-2-7

MARCINSON PRESS

10950-60 San Jose Blvd., Suite 136
Jacksonville, FL 32223 USA
editor@marcinsonpress.com
http://www.marcinsonpress.com

http://www.crunchtimelanguage.com
http://www.facebook.com/crunchtimelanguage

a special thank you

This book would not have been possible without Jenny Dulaney, who not only provided translations and voiced the audio, but also helped to guide us through the language nuances of Chinese parent-child relationships.

Wǒ hěn gǎn xiè!

The {NEW} Crunch-Time Guide to Parenting Language for Chinese Adoption

How to Use this Book

Teachers open the door.
You enter by yourself.
       - Chinese proverb

Ni hao! (Hello!) The New Crunch-Time Guide to Parenting Language for Chinese Adoption is designed to help parents be able to communicate effectively from day one. It's also great if you're already home and need to communicate quickly.

how it's organized

The book's sections are divided into simple categories, each color-coded so you can quickly find and dive into the section needed at any given moment. Within each section, words are listed in the general order of importance and frequency of usage – usually words first, common phrases last.

Sometimes, the English version of a phrase may seem a little odd. Why? We translated phrases as they're most commonly used as adult to child in China, which doesn't always have a direct word-for-word correlation in English. For instance, in the Western world we might say, "time for bed" but in China adults would say, "come to sleep." In the spirit of easier communication, we've used the Chinese phrasing the children are most likely used to hearing, rather than the English phrase.

why we included pinyin

Pinyin is a system of Romanization that enables everyone to read and write Mandarin without using traditional Chinese characters. We have included the pinyin for those familiar with it, but for those who aren't or who are struggling, we've created a pseudo-phonetic version of each word to serve as a guide.

learning the language tones

Part of the difficulty for those learning to speak Mandarin (Chinese) is learning the language's "tones" — the inflection of a syllable that can radically alter the word's meaning. There are four main tones:

 FIRST TONE For the first tone, you elongate the word. Think of it as kind of like saying "Aaaah" at the doctor. It is written like a long vowel mark: ā.

 SECOND TONE Inflection rises — kind of like when we ask a one word question in English. Pretend your friend has just informed you your favorite rock star is sitting in the local Starbucks. You would say in surprise, "Who?" It is written á to indicate the rise in the tone.

 THIRD TONE Inflection dips and then rises — kind of the way we instruct for breathing during exercise, "i-i-n, o-o-u-t, i-i-n, o-o-u-t, i-i-n, o-o-u-t." It is written like the short vowel sound to indicate the dip and rise: ǎ.

 FOURTH TONE For the fourth tone, the inflection technically falls, but the easiest way to understand it is to think of it as a command tone — kind of the way you would say "Stop!" to someone annoying you. It is written à to show that the tone falls.

as close as you can get

Mandarin (Chinese) and pinyin can also sometimes be confusing because the letters do not make the same sounds we are used to, and there are consonant blends we aren't used to seeing.

For example, "x" is pronounced "sh" in pinyin, and the zh is pronounced as a "j" sound. Very different than American English! To help you be better understood, we've created a pseudo-phonetic translation. Regardless of the pinyin spelling, we've written it the way you would expect to say it, using common English words whenever possible. We've added hyphens when syllables should be spoken together quickly, and have given the closest approximation we could get. For example, how would you pronounce the pinyin phrase "zhěn tóu"? The zh is pronounced as a "j", the e is pronounced like our word "uh" and tou is pronounced like our word, "toe." Hence, our pseudo-phonetic language helps you to pronounce it correctly just as we have written: "juhn toe."

English

:······· **pillow**   *zhěn tóu* ············:   *Pinyin*

juhn toe ············:

Sounds Like

Some sounds just don't translate well. Don't worry about it too much. You've got the basics here, and if you'd like to practice, we offer free audio files so you can actually hear the words spoken in Chinese (see page 39). With a little practice, you'll sound close enough that your child will understand you!

Day One

you are safe

nǐ shì ānquán de
knee sure an-chwuhn duh

it's okay

méi guān xì
may gwahn she

what do you want?

nǐ yào shénme?
knee yaow shun-mah?

show me

zhǐ gěi wǒ kàn
juh gay wuh kahn

you are going to live with us

nǐ jiang hé wǒmen zhù zài yìqǐ
**knee jee-yahng huh wuh-mun
joo dz-eye ee-chee**

we will take good care of you

wǒmen huì hǎo hǎo ge zhào gù nǐ

wuh-mun hway haow haow guh jaow goo knee

we will be your family

wǒmen jiānghui chéngwéi nǐ de jiātíng

wuh-mun jee-yahng-hway chung-hway knee duh jee-yah-teeng

car ride

zùo chē

dzwoh-uh chuh

We have included this sentence for parents in case needed during conversation with Chinese adults.

airplane ride

zuò fēijī

dzwoh-uh fay-jee

this is our adopted child

zhè shì wǒmen lǐngyǎng xiáo hái

juh sure wuh-mun leeng-yahng shee-yaow high

Immediate Family

mommy	*māmā* **mah-mah**	
daddy	*bàba* **bah-bah**	
sister	older sister *jiějie* **jee-yeh jee-yeh**	younger sister *mèimei* **may-may**
brother	older brother *gēgē* **guh-guh**	younger brother *dìdi* **dee-dee**
daughter	*nǚ'ér* **new-are**	
son	*érzi* **are-dzuh**	

Immediate Family

I am your mommy

wǒ shì nǐ de māmā
wuh sure knee duh mah-mah

I am your daddy

wǒ shì nǐ de bàba
wuh sure knee duh bah-bah

you are my daughter

nǐ shì wǒ de nǚ'ér
knee sure wuh duh new-are

you are my son

nǐ shì wǒ de érzi
knee sure wuh duh are-dzuh

Immediate Family

this is your older sister

zhè shì nǐ de jiějie
juh sure knee duh jee-yeh jee-yeh

this is your younger sister

zhè shì nǐ de mèimei
juh sure knee duh may-may

this is your older brother

zhè shì nǐ de gēgē
juh sure knee duh guh-guh

this is your younger brother

zhè shì nǐ de dìdi
juh sure knee duh dee-dee

Family & Friends

grandma	Dad's Mom	Mom's Mom
	năi nai	*wài pó*
	nigh nigh	**why pwoh-uh**

grandpa	Dad's Dad	Mom's Dad
	ye ye	*wài gōng*
	yeah yeah	**why gohng**

friend	*péngyŏu*
	puhng-yo

teacher	*lăoshī*
	lao-sure

this is our dog
zhè shì wŏmen de gŏu
juh sure wuh-mun duh gaow

this is our cat
zhè shì wŏmen de māo
juh sure wuh-mun duh maow

Feelings/Reassurance

hug
bào bao
baow baow

kiss
qīn qīn
cheen cheen

I love you
wǒ ài nǐ
wuh eye knee

are you sad?
nǐ nánguò ma?
knee nan-gwoh-uh mah?

are you angry?
nǐ shēngqì ma?
knee shuhng-chee mah?

I will help you
wǒ huì bāng nǐ
wuh hway bahng knee

Feelings/Reassurance

are you afraid?

nǐ hàipà ma?
knee high-pah mah?

don't be afraid

bùyào hàipà
boo-yaow high-pah

are you worried?

nǐ dānxīn ma?
knee dahn-sheen mah?

don't worry

bùyào dānxīn
boo-yaow dahn-sheen

I'll be right back

wǒ mǎshàng huílái
wuh mah-shahng hway-lye

I will come back soon

wǒ huì hěn kuài huílái
wuh hway hun kwhy hway-lye

 # Eating & Drinking

hungry *è*
uh

---

thirsty *kě*
kuh

---

bottle *nǎi píng*
nigh peeng

---

water *shuǐ*
shway

---

milk *níú nǎi*
knee-oh nigh

---

juice *gǔozhī*
gwoh-juh

---

eat *chī*
chure

Eating & Drinking

are you thirsty?

nǐ kě ma?

knee kuh mah?

are you hungry?

nǐ è ma?

knee uh mah?

more

duō yi diǎn

dwoh-uh ee dee-yen

finished

hǎo le

haow luh

we will have more later

wǒmen yǐ hòu hái huì yǒu de

wuh-mun ee ho high hway yo duh

Personal Care

bathroom	*cè sǔo*	**tsuh swoh**
bath	*xǐ zǎo*	**she dzaow**
diaper	*niàobù*	**knee-yaow boo**
pee pee	*niào niào*	**knee-yaow knee-yaow**
poo poo (for younger kids)	*biàn biàn*	**bee-yen bee-yen**

do you have to use the bathroom?

nǐ yào bú yào shàng cè sǔo
**knee yaow boo yaow shahng
tsuh swoh**

Personal Care

wash your hands
xǐshǒu
she-show

come take a bath/shower
lái xǐ zǎo
lie she dzaow

come brush your teeth
lái shuāyá
lie shwah-yah

come get dressed
lái chuān yīfú
lie chwuhn ee-foo

come brush your hair
lái shū tóu
lie shoe toe

Sleeping

bed	*chuáng* **chwahng**
blanket	*tǎn zi* **tahn juh**
pillow	*zhěn tóu* **juhn toe**

Just a reminder...
be sure you're
practicing! Some of
these words can be
difficult. Hear the
pronunciations for
yourself on our web
page. See page
39 for details.

come to sleep (go to bed)

lái shùi jiào
lie shway jee-yaow

go to sleep

qù shùi jiào
choo shway jee-yaow

please stay in your bed

liú zài nǐ de chuángshàng
leo dz-eye knee duh chwahng-shahng

Health & Medical

do you hurt?

nǐ téng ma?
knee tuhng mah?

where are you hurt?

nǐ nǎli téng?
knee naw-lee tuhng?

stuffy nose

bí sāi
be sigh

sore throat

hóulóng téng
ho-lohng tuhng

band-aid

chuàngkǒutiē
chwuhng-koh-tee-yeh
-or-
OK Beng
OK Bahng

Health & Medical

earache	*ěrduo téng* **are-dwoh-uh tuhng**
fever	*fāshāo* **fah-shaow**
headache	*tóu téng* **toe tuhng**
rash	*zhěnzi* **jen-juh**
toothache	*yá téng* **yah tuhng**
itching	*yǎng* **yahng**
diarrhea	*lā dùzi* **lah doo-juh**

Safety & Instruction

which one?
nǎ yī gē?
nigh ee guh?

let's play
wǒmen lái wán
wuh-mun lie wahn

let's go
wǒmen qù
wuh-mun choo

stop
tíng xià lái
teeng she-yah lie

stop now!
tíng!
teeng!

come here
lái
lie

sit down
zuò xià
dzwoh-uh she-yah

Safety & Instruction

do you need help?

nǐ xūyào bāngzhù ma?
knee shoe-yaow bahng-joo mah?

can you do it yourself?

nǐ kěyǐ zìjǐ zuò ma?
knee kuh-yee juh-jee dzwoh-uh mah?

I will help you

wǒ huì bāng nǐ
wuh hway bahng knee

that is not allowed

bù kě yǐ
boo kuh ee

this is very dangerous

zhè shì hěn wéixiǎn
juh sure hun way-shee-yen

Safety & Instruction

please don't hit

qǐng bùyào dǎ
cheeng boo-yaow dah

please don't kick

qǐng bùyào tī
cheeng boo-yaow tee

please don't bite

qǐng bùyào yǎo
cheeng boo-yaow yaow

please stop screaming

qǐng bùyào jiào
cheeng boo-yaow jee-yaow

please don't shout

qǐng bùyào hǎn
cheeng boo-yaow hahn

Safety & Instruction

please don't cry

qǐng bùyào kū
cheeng boo-yaow koo

you need to behave

nǐ yào guāi
knee yaow gwhy

you need to listen to mommy

nǐ yào tīng māmā
knee yaow teeng ma-ma

you need to listen to daddy

nǐ yào tīng bàba
knee yaow teeng bah-bah

stay by me

zài wǒ páng biān
dz-eye wuh pahng bee-yen

Manners

please	*qǐng* **cheeng**
thank you	*xièxie* **she-yeh she-yeh**
you're welcome	*bié kèqì* **bee-uh kuh-chee**
hello	*nǐ hǎo* **knee haow**
goodbye	*zàijiàn* **dz-eye jee-yen**
excuse me	*duìbùqǐ* **doo-ee boo-chee**

Colors

Red	*hóng sè*	**hohng suh**
blue	*lán sè*	**lawn suh**
yellow	*huáng sè*	**hwahng suh**
green	*lǜ sè*	**loo suh**
brown	*kāfāi sè*	**caw-fay suh**
purple	*zǐ sè*	**gee-yuh suh**
black	*hēi sè*	**hay suh**
white	*bái sè*	**bye suh**

Numbers

one	*yī*	**ee**
two	*èr*	**are**
three	*sān*	**sahn**
four	*sì*	**suh**
five	*wǔ*	**woo**
six	*liù*	**leo**
seven	*qī*	**chee**
eight	*bā*	**bah**
nine	*jiǔ*	**jo**
ten	*shí*	**shuh**

Music

Twinkle Twinkle Little Star

yī shǎn yī shǎn liàng jīng jīng
mǎn tiān dōu shì xiǎo xīngxing
guà zài tiānkōng fàng guāngmíng
hāoxiàng xǔduō xiǎo yǎnjīng
yī shǎn yī shǎn liàng jīng jīng
mǎn tiān dōu shì xiǎo xīngxing

Ee shawn ee shawn lee-ahng jeeng jeeng
Mahn tee-yan dough sure she-yaow sheeng-sheeng
Gwah dz-eye tee-yan-kohng fahng gwahng-meeng
How-she-yahng shoe dough she-yaow yan-jeeng
Ee shawn ee shawn lee-ahng jeeng jeeng
Man tee-yan dough sure she-yaow sheeng-sheeng

Although the Chinese version of this song doesn't translate word for word, the meaning is relatively close.

Music

Two Tigers
(Tune of Frère Jacques)

Liǎng zhī lǎohǔ
Liǎng zhī lǎohǔ
Pǎo de kuài
Pǎo de kuài
Yī zhī méiyǒu ěrduo
Yī zhī méiyǒu wěibā
Zhēn qíguài
Zhēn qíguài

Lee-ahng juh laow-who
Lee-ahng juh laow-who
Pow duh kwhy
Pow duh kwhy
Ee-juh mayo are-dwoh-uh
Ee-juh mayo way-bah
Jen chee-gwhy
Jen chee-gwhy

This is a well-known
Chinese children's song
that describes two
tigers running fast,
one has an ear missing,
one has a tail missing.

◁)) Hear it for yourself!

Keep in mind that when learning Mandarin under crunch conditions, practice will make progress, but it likely won't make perfect. That's okay. The idea behind this book is to give you some very basic survival language. You need just enough to be useful to you and your child until you are better able to communicate in English. If you then want to learn more, there are an enormous number of resources available.

Even with our pseudo-phonetic system, however, without the ability to say at least some of the words with the correct tones, it's possible your child still won't understand you. It really is important to practice. This is where our free audio files can be of assistance.

Visit our website:

http://www.crunchtimelanguage.com/485083721-2

The page will open to a chart with each of the individual words and phrases listed.

Happy listening and speaking!

Other adoption-related books published by Marcinson Press:

Awakening East: Moving our Adopted
Children Back to China

Geezer Dad: How I Survived Infertility Clinics,
Fatherhood Jitters, Adoption Wait Limbo,
and Things That Go "Waaa" in the Night

Are You Ready to Adopt? An Adoption
Insider's Look from the Other Side of the Desk

Ladybug Love: 100 Chinese Adoption
Match Day Stories

The New Crunch-Time Guide to
Parenting Language for Haitian Adoption

Available through Amazon.com and by request
through most major and independent bookstores.

MARCINSON PRESS

Made in the USA
Coppell, TX
15 September 2020

38117102R00026